Blenheim Palace: The History and Legacy of the Only Non-Royal Palace in England

By Charles River Editors

An 18th century engraving that depicts the Grand Court of the palace

About Charles River Editors

Charles River Editors provides superior editing and original writing services across the digital publishing industry, with the expertise to create digital content for publishers across a vast range of subject matter. In addition to providing original digital content for third party publishers, we also republish civilization's greatest literary works, bringing them to new generations of readers via ebooks.

Sign up here to receive updates about free books as we publish them, and visit Our Kindle Author Page to browse today's free promotions and our most recently published Kindle titles.

Introduction

Blenheim Palace

By the start of the 18th century, England had recovered from one of the most tumultuous periods in its history and was heading into the future with a new sense of unity. The civil wars were over, and despite some royals' unpopular tendency toward Catholicism and absolutism, the House of Stuart had survived the beheading of Charles I and the overthrow of James VII and II. William and Mary brought a period of reconciliation and stability in which William's interests on the continent led him to make concessions to Parliament, concessions that helped hold the nation together. Following the deaths of Mary in 1694 and William in 1702, the throne was inherited by Mary's sister, Anne. Under Anne, the Kingdoms of England and Scotland, previously united under the Stuarts' rule, were formally united as a nation. The Acts of Union of 1707 created a single kingdom, that of Great Britain.

At the same time, the "political union" also meant a union of the armed forces, and though both developments had been happening informally in the preceding years, they were now made official. Moving forward, there would be a British nation, and just as the nation was uniting, its armies came under the leadership of John Churchill, the 1st Duke of Marlborough, one of the most outstanding generals in British history.

John Churchill was born in 1650 into a noble family from Devon in the south of England. His father, Sir Winston Churchill, had sided with the Royalists in the civil wars, and the fines he had to pay for this left the family relatively poor by English aristocratic standards. The restoration of the monarchy in 1660 went some ways to boosting the family's fortunes. Over the following years, Churchill married and began raising a family. He alternated military and political service, meeting and impressing William of Orange during his diplomatic work on the continent. His rising military rank, social standing, and wealth made him a figure of prominence in Britain.

In 1685, Churchill's longstanding patron became King James II and VII. In turn, King James II and VII made Churchill the Baron Churchill of Sandridge, with a seat in the House of Lords. Churchill's military successes would also earn him the title of Duke of Marlborough, and after the victorious Battle of Blenheim, one of England's greatest residences was to be built for him to commemorate the success.

The English Baroque jewel in Oxfordshire, known to the locals as the fabled Blenheim Palace, is without question one of the finest buildings in the country, and even those who have never been there in person have likely seen it at some point or another in passing. The stunning structure has been photographed and documented countless times, and it can be seen in the backdrop of numerous international blockbuster hits, including *Harry Potter and the Order of the Phoenix, The Avengers, The Four Feathers, Gulliver's Travels, Lord of the Apes,* and *The Legend of Tarzan*, to name a few.

This majestic manor, the only non-royal estate in England to be categorized as a palace, is far more than just an attractive landmark. In fact, it is a place with enough history to fill an endless number of books. *Blenheim Palace: The History and Legacy of the Only Non-Royal Palace in England* examines the estate's architectural history, the toxic friendship that nearly upended the entire project, and the historic events that transpired within the palace's walls. Along with pictures of important people, places, and events, you will learn about the Blenheim Palace like never before.

Blenheim Palace: The History and Legacy of the Only Non-Royal Palace in England

About Charles River Editors

Introduction

    A Transcendent Tribute

    Scandals

    A House Is Not a Home

    A Legacy Like No Other

    Online Resources

    Further Reading

Free Books by Charles River Editors

Discounted Books by Charles River Editors

A Transcendent Tribute

Blenheim Palace

"I have not time to say more, but to beg you will give my duty to the Queen, and let her know Her army has had a Glorious Victory..." – excerpt from John Churchill's letter to his wife, Sarah, August 13, 1704

Upon first glance, the Dean Jones Room of the Blenheim Palace, most famed for having served as the birthplace of none other than British Prime Minister Winston Churchill, resembles a posh grandmother's bedchamber. The unmarked, cozy room, situated just off the majestic Great Hall, features a single double-bed robed in lacy white sheets atop a baroque rug in teal and eggshell-white, and is decorated with royal-red carpets, rose-print wallpapers, a velvet-cushioned rocking chair, a porcelain tea set, and a fine selection of oil paintings.

Every evening at 6:00 p.m., all members of the public are promptly escorted out of the premises and invited to return at 9:00 a.m. the following morning. The lights are then dimmed, and security is dispatched for their daily rounds. The task set before them is rather arduous, but relatively straightforward, yet many, they say, dread the night shifts. It is not the thieves, nor the vandals that make their guts squirm, but rather the terrifying trespassers from the beyond. Among its most frequent otherworldly visitors is Dean Jones, a former chaplain to John and Sarah Churchill, the 1st Duke and Duchess of Marlborough. The somber and shadowy ghost of the elderly spirit, say those who have witnessed him, paces back and forth, as if admiring the paintings mounted onto the wall, and as if trapped in an endless loop.

Dean Jones is only one in the palace's lengthy list of late-night phantom visitors. In the bedchamber just a few doors away, one may chance upon an unnamed Roundhead soldier from the Civil War era. This frightening figure – his silhouette made even more eerie by his distinctive dented helmet, reminiscent of a round cap fitted with a neck shade – is often seen either crumpled next to or hovering over the unlit fireplace. Peek out the window, if one dares, and one might catch a glimpse of the Fair Rosamund Clifford, the ravishing red-headed mistress of King Henry II. This entrancing, but tortured soul, whom many believe died by her own hand, can be seen floating across the verdant, immaculately manicured grass of the Blenheim Palace Park & Gardens, her reflection absent from the glass-like surface of its lake. Under the silvery discs of full moons, one might also catch her bathing in the square-shaped well, the spirit's namesake.

Still, these quiet apparitions, while deeply unsettling, are no more than unconventional, but otherwise respectful neighbors when juxtaposed with the perverse poltergeist that haunted Oliver Cromwell's royal commissioners in the autumn of 1649. As the story goes, selected commissioners were instructed to enter and temporarily occupy Woodstock Manor on the 13th of October, a sort of predecessor and soon-to-be component of the Blenheim Palace. There, they were to spend the following weeks packing up what was left of King Charles I's belongings, so as to eliminate all evidence of his tenure here. Alas, they could remain in the haunted manor for no more than 20 days.

On the very first evening, the commissioners found it difficult to drift off to sleep, but ultimately chalked it up to their unfamiliarity with the environment. But for a handful of these commissioners, shut-eye the following evening would be little more than a dream. In the still of the night, two commissioners claimed, the door to their bedroom creaked open, and in came a ghastly "phantom canine." The commissioners quickly shook the rest of their slumbering staff awake, all of whom later claimed to have watched the dog tear into the "cords" with its terrible teeth.

Unfortunately, the dog soon proved to be the least of their problems. A demonic spirit, the commissioners insisted, dwelt in, and therefore, presided over the manor – one they dubbed the "Royalist Devil of Woodstock." A few evenings later, the diabolical poltergeist heaved up and shook the beds of the commissioners relentlessly for several minutes; the spirit was supposedly so aggressive that his victims awoke the next morning covered in fresh bruises. To make matters worse, the commissioners stumbled into the dining hall only to find it in absolute disarray – chairs were overturned, and the pile of wood they had chopped the previous night was littered across the floor.

On the 29th of October, the commissioners were once again yanked from their light slumbers by the quaking floors and walls, and the shattering of the glass windows. Residents who lived nearby reported the alarming noises that came from Woodstock Manor that evening. The tension and fright-induced delirium amongst the shaken commissioners and their staff only climbed with each passing day. One of the servants came close to losing his life, nearly killed not by the Royalist Devil, but another servant, who panicked upon seeing what appeared to be a floating white nightgown in the middle of the night.

The living occupants of the manor began to arm themselves fruitlessly with swords, clubs, heavy pans, and other blunt objects before slipping into bed, but the straw heap that was their patience was fast dwindling. Meanwhile, the Royalist Devil continued to make his intentions clear, tossing furniture about, destroying more priceless, fragile items, snuffing out candles, and even dousing the unsuspecting commissioners with the contents of their chamber pots. Finally, sweet radio silence dominated for about two days, but on the 2nd of November, the Royalist Devil returned with a vengeance. Deafening bangs and guttural howls could be heard from three different locations within the manor. The sounds, said the commissioners, were so horrifying that it frightened off a couple of poachers who were attempting to jimmy their way through one of the rear entrances, the would-be thieves leaving behind their weapons and tools in their haste. Moments later, one of the commissioners spotted a disembodied hoofed leg, bent back as if preparing to stamp out the flame of his candle. The commissioner unsheathed his sword, but the Devil wrestled away his weapon with his "invisible hands," and sent him flying through the air and crashing unto the ground. And that was the final straw; the commissioners and servants, clearly having overstayed their welcome, filed out of the manor the next morning, vowing never to set foot in the haunted abode again. As one commissioner put it, "All the fiends of hell had been let loose on [us]."

In June 2017, the *BBC* reported that stonemasons had unearthed a series of peculiar vaults whilst remodeling the northern steps of the Blenheim Palace, which served as a stabilizing foundation for the small staircase. It was the second "surprise discovery" of the year; just three months earlier, an old flowerpot in the palace garden was identified as a 1,700-year-old Roman sarcophagus chiseled out of white marble. The re-purposed coffin, measuring about 6.6 feet across and weighing close to 882 lbs, was first installed as part of a fountain by the 5th Duke of Marlborough in the 19th century. The coffin, now worth an estimated £300,000, depicts an inebriated Dionysus, joined by Ariadne, Hercules, a pair of lion heads, and other deities. The discovery of the coffin was to many a missing piece of the paranormal puzzle that lies within the palace, the source of all its inexplicable occurrences.

As intriguing and entertaining as alleged ghost stories are, they pale in comparison to the actual history behind and within the Blenheim Palace, a 2,000-acre property boasting 187 rooms that has become an irreplaceable landmark. Indeed, it is the only non-royal, non-episcopal country house recognized as a palace in all of England, and it owes its existence to one of Britain's most renowned military heroes.

John Churchill, the 1st Duke of Marlborough, was without question, one of the most controversial figures of his era, even as he has been eulogized by many chroniclers as "Britain's finest general." Richard Holmes, for instance, wrote that he "bore a greater burden, military and political, than any commander before or since, and of him alone could it be said that he never besieged a town he did not take, or fought a battle he did not win." That being said, to simply reduce him to a capable general would be to disregard his lesser-known, but nevertheless noteworthy achievements.

John, born in 1650, came from humble beginnings. He was the younger son of Winston and Elizabeth Churchill, the former a mid-level commoner who owned a small chunk of land. Prestige was not what one would associate with the family name, and the lineage's status was further hindered by the patriarch's decision to support the losing Royalists during the Civil War. Among the consequences Winston faced was a debilitating fine of £4,446 (roughly £582,600 in purchasing power today). Still, the prudent patriarch taught his children to keep their chins lifted no matter the circumstance, coining the tongue-in-cheek family motto that continues to be in use to this day: "Fiel Pero Desdichado" (Faithful, but Unfortunate").

John cherished the life lessons imparted unto him, but he was eager to elevate his personal status and, in turn, that of the family name. Some might call him a "social climber," one happy to ride the coattails of his best contacts so as to improve upon his personal quality of life. As a young man, he used his sister Arabella's friendship with the Duke of York and future King James II as a stepping stone to nab a position as a royal page, and he eventually received a post in the First Foot Guards. Taking advantage of his lowly, but promising posts, John built and strengthened a profound relationship with the Duke of York himself, and at the age of 28, he took Sarah Jennings, one of Princess (later Queen) Anne's ladies-in-waiting, as his bride.

John Churchill

King James II

With the Duke of York on his side, John rapidly scaled the ranks. James was fascinated by the military, and Churchill took up his patron's obsession. In 1767, he became an ensign in the King's Own Company in the 1st Guards. As a member of the Guards, he was posted to sea several times, serving as a marine on British ships. He also fought on a British warship at the Battle of Solebay in 1672.

Soon after Solebay, Churchill was made a captain in the Duke of York's Admiralty Regiment. He fought at the Siege of Maastricht in 1673, where he was part of a successful forlorn hope, one of the groups of daring soldiers who stormed defenses. During the fighting, he saved the life of the Duke of Monmouth, for which he was praised by the Stuarts and the French King Louis XIV.

By 1685, the year of King James II's coronation, John, at this stage a lieutenant-general, had become a prominent member of the king's retinue. In turn, King James II and VII made Churchill the Baron Churchill of Sandridge, with a seat in the House of Lords. Churchill subsequently played a leading role in suppressing the revolt against James by Charles II's illegitimate son, the Duke of Monmouth, which earned Churchill the rank of Major General.

At first, when Parliament invited William of Orange to take the British throne in 1688, Churchill remained loyal to King James, but as support for the monarch faded away, it became clear that the future lay with William and Mary. Within three weeks, Churchill had defected to William's side, taking hundreds of officers and men with him. Unable to retain the loyalty even of a man he had made, James fled and war was averted.

An engraving of William & Mary

John had become increasingly wary of the Roman Catholic monarch's vehement campaign against the Protestants, and as such, he took the side of William of Orange, James' very own son-in-law. For his efforts in what is now remembered as the "Glorious Revolution of 1688," which resulted in the deposition of James II, the ascendancy of King William III, and the restoration of Protestantism in England, John was handsomely rewarded. John, who had been promoted to Baron in the Scottish peerage in 1682, followed by the English peerage three years later, was appointed Earl of Marlborough in 1689.

In the wake of that, he became a member of the Privy Council, the group of men who helped the royal couple run the country. He helped reform the army, building a patronage network centered around himself. During the Nine Years' War (1688–1697), he spent three years in the field, and though seldom in overall command, he earned praise from European colleagues at the Battle of Walcourt in 1689. In August 1690, he had his first independent command, leading a land and sea operation against Jacobite rebels in Ireland. Though it had lacked the drama he had hoped for, it was still a significant success.

Marlborough and his wife, Sarah, were lifelong courtiers and inveterate schemers. Their intrigue, along with Marlborough's ongoing contact with the exiled James II, eventually destroyed the trust between them and the king and queen. A forged letter led to Marlborough's imprisonment on charges of treason in 1692, but his name was cleared and he was released after five weeks. He was accused of betraying his country by warning James of a planned attack on the French city of Brest in 1694, though evidence of this remains inconclusive.

Sarah Churchill

Following Queen Mary's death in 1694, Marlborough and Sarah began to regain position at court. After years on the sidelines, he regained his military rank and position on the Privy Council in 1698, even as relations between Marlborough and King William remained cold.

The Earl of Marlborough continued to milk his relationships with the royals for all they were worth. In 1702, the year Queen Anne took the throne, John was named captain-general of the royal armies, deputy commander of Dutch forces, and the "master-general of the ordnance," and was further bumped up to "Duke of Marlborough" on Christmas Day that year, which came with a plump annual salary of £5,000.

The Duke of Marlborough would soon prove to be worth every penny of his ample salary. The death of Charles II of Spain in 1700 prompted a succession crisis, propelling Europe into a long, costly conflict. The war was sparked by the overzealous King Louis XIV's determination to broaden the French empire. Rival royals observed with bated breath the frayed rope that was the health of the heirless Spanish king, Charles II, tenuously held together by a flimsy thread. As such, the coveted throne was now potentially at the mercy of a trinity of contenders. There was King Louis, who hoped to gain the reins via his eldest son, Louis, the Grand Dauphin, whom he produced with Marie Therese (which made the Grand Dauphin the grandson of former Spanish King Philip IV). Then there was the Holy Roman Emperor Leopold I, once the husband of Margaret Theresa (another one of King Philip's daughters), who sought the throne on behalf of his son by a different wife (Eleanor Magdalene of Neuburg), the future Emperor Charles VI. Lastly, there was Joseph Ferdinand of Bavaria, the great-grandson of Philip IV.

Both Holland and England were dead set against the marriage of the Spanish and French territories. Not only would this propel France to the forefront of the continent's superpowers, the former nations could stand to lose substantial profits, for Spain was prepared to sever its commercial ties to them in favor of France. Moreover, Holland, England, and even France were inimical to the ascension of Leopold's son, then Archduke Charles, for such an event would strengthen the bonds between the Austrian and Spanish members of the Habsburg dynasty, posing a different set of threats to the current power structure.

Tensions continued to intensify, and on May 15, 1702, England called for war against France. As fate would have it, the War of the Spanish Succession (1701-1714) witnessed Marlborough's greatest achievements. Extolled by Holmes as "Eisenhower, Montgomery, and Brooke rolled into one," he was not only a competent fighter, but also a brilliant strategist who designed the remarkable plans of action that kept his unblemished track record on the battlefield intact. Saul David of *The Telegraph* noted that he "firmly grasped the essentials of the three combat arms, using infantry for firepower, cavalry for shock, and artillery to tilt the balance...Like all great captains, he knew the importance of 'solid training,' and no detail of logistics was beneath his attention. Moreover, he possessed that 'shamanistic quality' which enables a general to 'get straight to the hearts of the soldiers they command.'"

John was from the very beginning placed in charge of the British, Dutch, and supplementary German mercenaries, but despite his protests, his powers were restricted. He could only direct the Dutch troops if they were already "in action with his own." Executive decisions outside of this specific situation could only be made with the unanimous consent of the present Dutch officials. With this arrangement set in place, England, backed by Holland, Austria, and the better part of the German states went to battle against the opposing forces, which belonged to France, Spain, Portugal, Savoy, and Bavaria.

Between 1702 and 1703, John continuously butted heads with the Dutch. Even so, the practiced captain-general succeeded in his campaigns across the Low Countries. He exercised the tactics that aided in his triumphs, and absorbed lessons from his clashes with the Dutch officials, all of which paved the path to his victory at the Battle of Blenheim on August 13, 1704.

At this point, France, Bavaria, and Hungary had Austria cornered, leaving the Austrians with few other alternatives but to wave the white flag. Understanding the importance of keeping Emperor Leopold in the war, the Duke of Marlborough chose to extend his assistance to the Danube, but this was a dauntless move that took some scheming. He ordered his English soldiers to relocate to the department of Moselle in northeastern France, and from there, he would sidestep the Dutch and carry on southward to join forces with the Austrians in Germany.

With that, on August 13, 1704, the Duke of Marlborough and Prince Eugene brought the opposing Franco-Bavarian forces to their knees. Chronicler John Lynn would later call it "one of the greatest examples of marching and fighting before Napoleon." With the Duke's devious, but ultimately effective plan, Bavaria and Cologne had no choice but to admit defeat and quit the war. More importantly, England's success at the Battle of Blenheim smote the French kingdom with a destructive blow, one that King Louis XIV failed to recover from, thereby rendering him powerless to conquer the continent as the French sovereign had originally planned. The result freed up the British to enlarge their own empire and achieve what Louis' France had failed to accomplish.

A depiction of the duke at the battle

A scene from the Blenheim Tapestry on display at the palace

Having achieved what many now believe to be the glowing highlight of his military career, John was extolled by all his peers as the premier military commander of the British Empire. Even the Tories, who vowed to "break him up like hounds on a hare" should he fail to deliver, swallowed their pride and acknowledged the feat. Emperor Leopold was so grateful for the aid provided by the duke that he awarded him the title of "Prince of Mindelheim."

Above all, Queen Anne remained the Duke's most important admirer. In addition to the praises she lavished upon him, she presented him with the remnants of the then-defunct Woodstock Manor and its surrounding terrain in Oxfordshire, including the "tenancy of the royal manor of Hensington," as an undying token of her appreciation. There, John and his beloved wife were granted permission to transform the ruins to a regal private manor for the esteemed couple and all future Churchill descendants. The captain-general's personal palace was to be christened the "Blenheim Manor," later "Blenheim Palace," after his most celebrated victory.

Queen Anne

Members of Parliament were also thoroughly basking in the triumph, so much so that they dedicated £240,000 (approximately £36.33 million today) to the construction of the palace. As a formality, John and his descendants were obliged to pay rent, otherwise known as "petit serjeanty," for the land bestowed upon them, but because of his valiant efforts, the payment was honorary as opposed to monetary. On the 13th of August each year, the Churchill family was to officially submit to the English sovereign "one copy of the French royal flag."

The royal gardener, Henry Wise, prepped the site for construction, and at 6:00 p.m. on June 18, 1705, the sleek foundation stone, measuring 8 square feet, was laid just below the bow window. Two months later, more than 1,500 laborers were on site, clearing debris, piecing together building blocks, and hauling supplies from one point to another.

It was a strong start, but things were about to unravel almost before they could even begin.

Scandals

"And everybody praised the Duke

Who this great fight did win.

'But what good came of it at last?'...

'Why, that I cannot tell,' said he,

'But 'twas a famous victory.'" - "The Battle of Blenheim," 18th century poet, Robert Southey

11-year-old Sarah Jennings was first employed as a junior lady-in-waiting for the 6-year-old Princess-turned-Queen Anne in 1671, and it was then that the contrasting duo became fast friends. The attractive and effervescent Sarah, who was eventually upgraded to "First Lady of the Bedchamber," was far more than merely a handmaiden – she was the playmate and closest confidante of the sickly and often pallid princess. They were as different, but as compatible as night and day, a cryptic dynamic that was as paradoxically resilient as it was brittle. Anne Somerset, the author of the biography *Queen Anne: The Politics of Passion*, explained that the future queen "was very poorly educated and chronically shy. She was often in appalling ill-health – probably an auto-immune disease and a form of arthritis. But in some ways she coped well with the challenges." It was the charismatic and captivating Sarah who remained a constant in the princess' life, holding her hand as she conquered every obstacle that life presented to her.

The inseparable pair had a truly intimate relationship, one marked by soul-bearing secrets, inside jokes, and floods of tears. They invented nicknames for one another, with Anne becoming "Mrs. Morley" and Sarah known as "Mrs. Freeman." In addition to the endless letters exchanged between the pair, they even spoke in code when surrounded by "outsiders." Indeed, the girls were closer than most, but such borderline "romantic friendships" were not unheard of back in the day, for they were seen as a rite of passage of sorts that primed them for marriage.

When the 17-year-old Sarah married John in the winter of 1677, she and Anne remained closer than ever. The calculating Sarah would have certainly relied on her friendship with royalty to advance her husband's career.

The rest of the royals were initially delighted by the friendship between them, but over time, they became disconcerted by the clear influence the opinionated Sarah had on the impressionable princess. Furthermore, they were scandalized by what they believed to be overtly amorous language in their letters. One of Anne's letters to Sarah read, "I hope I shall get a moment or two to be with my dear...That I may have one dear embrace, which I long for more than I can express." Some chastised Anne for clinging desperately onto "an immoderate passion inappropriate for a princess," and they recommended that monarchs, officials, and attendants alike keep an eye on the cunning Sarah. Anne vigorously countered every complaint.

Anne's sister, Queen Mary II, demanded that the pair part ways for good, but again the persistent princess protested. It was Sarah, after all, who had supported her throughout her years of poor health, the pain she felt from having been ostracized by her family members, and her multiple miscarriages. In Anne's own words, "let them do what they please, nothing shall ever vex me, so I can have the satisfaction of seeing dear [Sarah], and I swear I would live on bread and water between four walls with her, without repining, for as long as you continue kind..."

Sarah added more fuel to the fire by urging Anne to demand a parliamentary annual salary of £50,000, which would render the princess "financially independent" from William and Mary. There was some pushback from the sovereigns, but they ultimately acquiesced. This event cemented Anne's loyalty to Sarah, for the former credited the latter with gifting her the independence she had so long desired.

Predictably, upon Anne's inheritance of the crown, Duchess Sarah soared to the top of the hierarchy with her. She was appointed Groom of the Stole, Mistress of the Robes, and Keeper of the Privy Purse, the three highest-ranking positions in Queen Anne's court. To top it all off, Sarah and John were to receive an annual pension of £60,000. Following the duke's victory at Blenheim, the palace in question was formally presented to the couple, as verified by the inscription engraved unto the East Gate: "Under the auspices of a munificent sovereign, this house was built for John Duke of Marlborough and his Duchess Sarah, by Sir J. Vanbrugh between the years 1705 and 1722. And this Royal manor of Woodstock, together with a grant of £240,000, towards the building of Blenheim was given by Her Majesty Queen Anne, and confirmed by Act of Parliament..." While Anne undoubtedly felt beholden to the duke for his services, some believe the palace was a tangible expression of the queen's love for her lifelong friend.

For more than two decades, Anne instinctively resisted anyone who dared speak ill of Sarah, but the queen's enabling of the "manipulative" duchess' behavior only further emboldened her. Slowly, but surely, even Anne herself was finding it difficult to see past Sarah's toxicity, and what began as valid, well-grounded advice turned into blatantly self-serving orders barked to the queen as if she was a commoner. Sarah, a champion of the Whig Party, badgered Anne with proposals for partisan laws and policies, and she threw tantrums when rejected. The rift between them grew wider yet when the older and wiser Anne began to consult with Tory representatives in confidence.

Perhaps sensing the inevitable demise of their relationship, Sarah spiraled further out of control. Their arguments multiplied, worsened, and escalated in pettiness. Sarah mocked Anne for her lack of fashion sense, once ridiculing the jewels the queen chose for the celebration of the duke's victory at the Battle of Oudenarde.

Whether Anne and Sarah were ever romantically involved continues to be a matter of dispute, but the duchess clearly had a vicious jealous streak, and it manifested itself in full form when Anne began to spend more time with Abigail Hill Masham, one of Sarah's younger relatives. Making things worse, it had been Sarah who had invited Abigail to Anne's court, which she hoped would conceal her cousin's "embarrassing" roots. This further incensed the duchess, who branded her cousin a "viper" and called her Queen Anne's "slute of state." Allegedly, the duchess even arranged for her secretary, Arthur Maynwaring, to concoct fictitious and malicious pamphlets and ballads that alluded to the "immoral" lesbian nature of Anne and Abigail's relationship. One such ballad described the "sweet service" and "dark deeds at night" that Abigail supposedly performed for Anne after hours.

The length and theatrical nature of the bickering friends' very public conflicts continued to heighten, but it was the death of Anne's husband, George, in 1708 that many say upended the friendship once and for all. Sarah had attempted to dictate Anne's mourning process, and it was then, they say, that the queen finally snapped.

Others, however, claim it was a more political event that irreparably fractured the friendship. Not long after the rows triggered by George's death, Sarah pestered Anne about promoting her son-in-law, Charles Spencer (a registered Whig), to Privy Councilor. To this, Anne objected, but once again, Sarah twisted her arm until she relented, all the while shoving her Whig ideologies down the queen's throat. Following a particularly tempestuous altercation, a weeping Anne reportedly confided in Lord Godolphin that their friendship was over.

Despite the multiple warnings issued to the mulish Duchess, Sarah continued to skate on thin ice with the queen, and the ice cracked in 1711. That year, the disgraced Duke and Duchess of Marlborough were dishonorably discharged from court, and they had to surrender the golden key, which represented the lofty titles and signified the stripping of all her titles. Funding for the construction of the Blenheim Palace itself was immediately frozen, leaving the unfinished structure in limbo.

For his part, the duke could do little to remedy the situation, for there were all kinds of accusations leveled against him. He was castigated for his spendthrift habits, his excessive appetite for power, and the fickleness and duplicity of his character. On top of the duke's irresponsible money management (one historian described his personal expenditures as "rapacity remarkable even in a rapacious age"), the duke was also accused of embezzling funds set aside for the payment of foreign mercenaries, as well as accepting bribes for military contracts. Proof of the crimes, some say, rested in their alleged hoarding of jewels.

Alienated from Queen Anne, unpopular with the government, and better connected with Britain's continental allies than with leaders at home, the duke was relieved of all important positions by the end of 1711. Britain's allies were stunned, while France, their main opponent, was relieved at the removal of one of the main obstacles to its peace negotiations. As the Duke of Marlborough toured the courts of Europe, Britain negotiated a peace that left the nation in a position of unprecedented dominance, all of which had been made possible by his military successes. Meanwhile, construction of the Blenheim Palace would not be restarted until the day after the queen's death on August 1, 1714.

Perhaps not surprisingly, the selection process that aimed to narrow down a master architect for the palace was also riddled with controversy. Of course, Sarah, who was never one to bite her tongue, made her perfect candidate known. Her choice was Sir Christopher Wren, most famed for redesigning St. Paul's Cathedral, the stupendous all-ivory monument dedicated to the Anglican faith, back in 1669. Sir Wren was also later commissioned to design the Marlborough House, another gift from the queen that had been completed in 1711. Wren almost never disagreed with the irritable duchess, and he followed her instructions without complaint, designing for her a quaintly rustic, yet spacious brick building based on her specific request of function over form.

Sir Wren

The Marlborough House

John, on the other hand, regarded the gift as a tribute to his military achievements, and as such, he asserted that he alone be involved in the hiring process. It's easy to imagine Sarah's rage when she learned that her husband had given away the position without first consulting her, and she must have been even madder when she discovered that John's candidate, Mr. John Vanbrugh, was only minimally experienced in the field of architecture. The Duke had happened upon the charming Vanbrugh, a dramatist by trade, at a playhouse.

Vanbrugh

No more than an hour into their conversation, the enterprising Vanbrugh invited the duke to view Castle Howard in North Yorkshire. Then in its preliminary stages, it would become a stately Baroque manor and estate that would one day span over 13,000 acres, and it was the muse behind the Blenheim Palace. The duke seemed unconcerned about the fact that Vanbrugh had yet to complete what was his first venture into architecture, and promptly after the viewing, he awarded the position to Vanbrugh on the spot. Vanbrugh was to be assisted by his partner, Nicholas Hawkmoor. Hawksmoor was a protégé of Sarah's preferred candidate, which was most likely what led to the duchess' ultimate acceptance of her husband's decision. Master woodcarver and stone sculptors Grinling Gibbons and Edward Strong I, most renowned for their masonry in

Windsor Castle and Winchester Palace, respectively, were employed soon thereafter and tasked with the design and execution of the stonework on the palace facade and interior.

Castle Howard

Vanbrugh was nervous about the colossal endeavor that lay ahead of him, but he was also anxious to prove his worth. Much to his dismay, while Sarah had begrudgingly swallowed the bitter pill of hiring an unschooled builder as the palace's head architect, she had also proclaimed herself project manager, and she was resolved to make his life a living hell. Since her husband was often away, Vanbrugh had no choice but to answer to the Duchess.

Naturally, what the master architect and the self-proclaimed project manager envisioned for the country house were different from the very beginning. Vanbrugh, a conservationist at heart, fought to preserve the old ruins of Woodstock Manor and include it in the final design. He attempted to reason with Sarah, underscoring the importance of the 500-year-old manor's history. Woodstock, assembled under the instruction of the 12th-century monarch King Henry I, was girdled by a lush deer park inhabited by domesticated does, stags, lions, and porcupines. This was also where the king's mistress, Rosamund Clifford, and her miraculous well resided. Two centuries later, Woodstock served as the birthplace for King Edward III, the fabled "Black Prince," and between the years of 1554 and 1555, it doubled as a place of confinement for its sole prisoner, the future Queen Elizabeth I.

In spite of his best efforts, Vanbrugh's animated description of Woodstock's riveting history did nothing to sway the disinterested duchess. Instead, Sarah ordered the laborers to raze almost all of it to the ground, aside from recycling some of the fallen manor's foundations and rubble to reuse them in the new structure.

As the disagreements between Vanbrugh and Sarah continued, they created a progressively uncomfortable working environment for builders, artisans, and laborers alike, which, needless to say, slowed down the construction process. Vanbrugh remained adamant that Blenheim be designed as "a royal commission...[and] a monument to the Queen's glory, and a family home second." This infuriated the Duchess, especially given the disintegration of her friendship with the queen; some say her misplaced fury was kindled by a subconscious fear of what would soon be her fall from grace.

When the duke eventually retired from the battlefield, the frequency and increasing hostility of Sarah and Vanbrugh's quarrels became too much for him to handle. He made several attempts to mediate, but it was a losing battle, and eventually he merely asked that one wing of the construction site be left silent for his sake of his health and sanity.

Vanbrugh's exasperation with the duchess was captured in the letters he penned and later published. One excerpt, a letter addressed to Sarah, reads, "These papers, Madam, are so full of far-fetched labored accusations, mistaken facts, wrong inferences, groundless jealousies, and strained constructions, that I should put a very great affront upon your understanding if I supposed it possible you could mean anything in earnest by them, but to put a stop to my troubling you anymore. You have your end, Madam, for I will never trouble you more, unless the Duke of Marlborough recovers so far to shelter me from such intolerable treatment."

Suffice it to say, the absence of the duke and duchess must have been something of a relief for Vanbrugh when the construction stalled in 1711. Though he was excited to revive the incomplete project less than three years later, part of him must have shuddered at the thought of the controversial couple's return. The personality of the shrewd and comely duchess was supposedly so repulsive that even her own daughters conjured up every excuse to avoid visiting her. Sarah herself seemed to be aware of her trenchant attitude towards work, once remarking, "I made Mr. Vanbrugh my enemy by the constant disputes I had with him to prevent his extravagance."

Once again, the duchess reinstated herself as project supervisor and reverted to her micromanaging tactics. Ironically, though she herself knew nothing about architecture, she managed to detect faults almost every step of the way. She reprimanded Vanbrugh for the "wild" and "unmerciful" design of the house, callously criticized the abilities of Vanbrugh's 1,500 laborers, and probingly policed and questioned the integrity of Vanbrugh's costs and transactions. Moreover, regardless of the fact that Sarah – who would amass 27 estates and a personal fortune worth £120 million by the time of her death – was far from hurting for money, she was notoriously stingy. Not only did the Duchess challenge even the most minute and easily explainable expenses, she controlled the bulk of the funds and at times refused to honor outstanding bills altogether. At one point, bills that amounted £45,000 were left unpaid.

The antipathy between the two came to a head in early November 1716. According to most accounts, their dispute was centered on the new names that the duchess took it upon herself to add to the growingly muddled roster, in particular James Moore, royal cabinet maker to the newly-crowned King George I. Vanbrugh tendered his resignation just hours after the climactic confrontation, and he was thenceforth banished from Blenheim Palace.

Following Vanbrugh's departure, Moore served as the provisional Clerk of Works, and he later passed the torch to Hawksmoor. Their laborers constructed the Triumphal Arch, the Long Library, and finished the first phase of the palace. Edward Strong and his son, Edward II, were placed in charge of the masonry. Sir James Thornhill, who was commissioned to fresco the ceilings of the Great Hall, originally had the ceilings of the library and salon as the next items on his agenda. When Sarah received the first bill, however, she accused him of fleecing her and replaced him with Louis Laguerre instead.

Vanbrugh was crushed by his failure to complete what he considered his magnum opus. In 1719, upon learning that the duchess was away on other business, the former architect snuck onto the construction site to observe its current state. He hoped that Sarah would one day lift the banishment against him, but the duchess was not one to forgive, let alone forget. Even his wife, Henrietta Yarborough of Yorkshire, was refused entry when the nearly completed palace was opened for public viewing in 1725.

A contemporary engraving of the palace

The Grand Bridge

The west façade of the palace

A House Is Not a Home

> "Thanks, Sir, cried I, 'tis very fine,
>
> But where do you sleep, or where d'ye dine?
>
> I find by all you have been telling,
>
> That 'tis a house, but not a dwelling."
>
> – Alexander Pope, 18th century poet on Blenheim Palace

When the 1st Duke of Marlborough dished out an extra £60,000 to fund the palace's construction back in 1705, he did so willingly. Upon the return of the once-discredited duke and duchess, accompanied by "a train of coaches and a troop of militia with drums and trumpets," however, they were left to fund what was left of the project out of their own pockets. Between the years of 1716 and 1720, the couple forked over an additional £32,000.

Following the death of the duke in 1722, the surviving duchess, who became driven to complete the country house in honor of her dearly departed husband, craftily paid just half of the £50,000 that John had devoted to the completion of Blenheim prior to his demise, or so she claimed. Sarah prided herself on her resourcefulness and penchant for bargains, or as Vanbrugh saw it, an almost admirable ability to cut corners. Salaries were slashed in droves, and the penny-pinching Duchess also opted for cheaper building materials of inferior quality in places she deemed to be inconspicuous to the naked eye.

All in all, Sarah maintained that the palace cost no more than £100,000 (approximately £15.79 million today). Most historians, on the other hand, beg to differ. Sarah's statement, they assert, would only ring true if numerous unsettled bills and a number of other pre-banishment expenditures were removed from the equation. A ballpark figure of the palace's actual costs, they say, is most likely closer to £325,000 (£51.31 million).

In 1723, Hawksmoor, who now spearheaded the project, began work on the Triumphal Arch, otherwise known as the "Arch of Triumph." There were two principal entrances to the palace. One was situated just south of the Woodstock ruins on Oxford Road, and the other, through the Arch of Triumph, led to Park Street. The entryway was modeled after the Roman Arch of Titus, which was raised by Domitian at the base of Palatine Hill in Rome's Via Sacra in 81 CE. The Blenheim's Roman counterpart was constructed to memorialize the conquests of Domitian's father, Vespasian, and his brother, Titus, during the First Jewish War. Similarly, the arch erected at Blenheim Palace was a plain, but elegant two-tiered structure with sharp, defined squares protruding from the corners of its roofs, shored up by smooth Corinthian pillars. The arch was dedicated to the duke's victory at the Battle of Blenheim, and it was completed in 1724, two years after his death.

Magnus Manske's picture of the arch

Three years later, Hawksmoor began the Column of Victory, a vertically fluted Doric pillar hewn out of limestone ashlar. At 131 feet tall, it is topped by a stunning lead statue of the 1st Duke of Marlborough. The war hero, garbed in the attire of a Roman general and surrounded by four mighty eagles underneath his pedestal, is depicted with a crown and cape, clutching the scepter of "Winged Victory" in his outstretched fist. The concept of the monument was initially conceived by Vanbrugh, but it was designed and carried into fruition by Hawksmoor, who was inspired by a similar monumental column in Rome. The stonemasons assigned to the column's execution were Oxford natives William Townesend and Bartholomew Peisley.

The Column of Victory

Three facets of the column, completed in 1730 at a cost of £3,000, feature engravings of selected passages from Acts of Parliament that pledged sole ownership of the estate to John Churchill and his descendants. On the remaining facet was a poetic epitaph devoted to the duke that was authored by Henry St. John, the 1st Viscount of Bolingbroke, one of John's former political rivals. The inscription reads:

"The Castle of Blenheim was founded by Queen Anne,

In the Fourth Year of her Reign...

A monument designed to perpetuate the Memory of the Signal Victory,

Obtained over the FRENCH and BAVARIANS.

Near the Village of BLENHEIM,

On the Banks of the DANUBE,

By JOHN, DUKE OF MARLBOROUGH:

The Hero not only of his Nation, but his Age...

Who by Wisdom, Justice, Candor, and Address,

Reconciled various and even opposite Interests...

Which united in one common Cause,

The Principal States of Europe...

[and] Rescued the EMPIRE from Desolation;

Asserted and confirmed the Liberties of Europe!"

   The construction of the Palace Chapel, which commenced in 1730, is now believed to have been the last major section of the palace that was completed before the duchess' death. In 1732, Sarah announced the unveiling of the manor's worshiping place, as revealed by a letter she wrote that year. It read, "The Chappel [sic] is finish'd and more than half the Tomb there ready to set up." The Blenheim Chapel was consecrated a year later.

Magnus Manske's picture of the couple's tomb in the chapel of the palace

Upon its completion, the duchess marveled at the polished, uncomplicated refinement that prevailed in the modestly adorned chapel. Its designer, William Kent, dutifully decorated the ceilings and walls with monotone Baroque accents and floral patterns that were only a shade or two darker than the rest of the chapel, so as to fit the duchess' preferences. The pews, organ, and supplementary statues were added much later.

The duke's body was first laid to rest in Westminster Abbey, but when Sarah died in October 1744 at the age of 84, she was buried underneath the Blenheim Palace Chapel. Soon thereafter, the duke was exhumed and relocated to Blenheim. His bones were then re-interred in compact crimson leather coffins and encased in an astounding white marble sarcophagus mottled with gorgeous gray veins. An imposing multi-layered stone sculpture crowned the duke's sarcophagus. Above are statues carved in the likenesses of the duke and duchess, seated upon ornamented thrones and dressed in Caesarian robes, and below them are a pair of winged angels bearing a scroll with a short elegy for them. A beautiful bas relief featuring the "Surrender of Marshal Tallard," as per the Duchess' request, was carved unto the base.

The Earl of Godolphin succeeded in his campaign to install the unadorned wooden altar against the west wall of the chapel, which was then strictly against Christian tradition, so as to allow the sarcophagus to serve as the centerpiece. The Spencer-Churchill family crest, a crowded emblem featuring a double-headed eagle, lions, a pair of red dragons with poisonous spikes on the tip of their tails, a snarling griffin, and the family motto ("Fiel pero desdichado") adorn the elaborate sarcophagus.

A precise date that marks the completion of the palace's first phase has yet to be agreed upon. Whereas some consider it to be 1733, the year of the Palace Chapel's consecration, others point out that the duchess had reportedly been quibbling with Flemish sculptor John Michael Rysbrack over the price of the Long Library's Queen Anne statue as late as 1735. What is certain, however, is that the commemorative themes paying homage to the duke were not fully realized until just shortly before Sarah's death in 1744.

Even in 1744, it would not be a stretch to hail Blenheim Palace as an authentic English Baroque masterpiece. Throughout its sprawling gardens, cobblestone paths, and hypnotic water terraces, symmetry and balance reigned throughout the towering manor's romantic exterior. The building was garnished with intricate bas reliefs, exquisite sculptures of men and beasts, small armies of Doric half-columns and Corinthian pillars, and an assortment of grilled windows. The "main block" of the palace accommodates a forecourt to its north, and it is extended by two symmetrical arms on either side of it: the kitchen and stable courts via colonnades. Belvederes, the slender, rectangular towers capped with a quartet of spires placed on all four corners of the main block, evened out the picture. Visitors will find similar belvederes attached to the kitchen and stable courts.

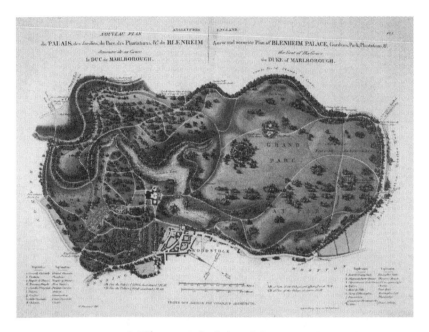

A 19th century depiction of the estate

The execution of this splendid and subtly regal facade, as one might imagine, was a task as arduous as it was satisfying. Sourcing the building blocks was an uphill battle itself. At first, Vanbrugh hoped to rely on the stone in the old park's four quarries. Only upon taking a closer look did it dawn on him that while the stone was fine and smooth, and could perhaps be used in the palace interior, it was far too delicate a material for the facade. As such, the building blocks for the palace exterior had to be brought in from 22 quarries in the Cotswolds, as well as Lord Rochester's quarry in Cornbury Estate. 136 men were needed to haul in the blocks from Taynton and Burford alone, which drove up the costs.

The following description, written by W. J. Arkell shortly after his visit in July of 1948, focuses on the building materials and gives readers a taste of the palace's striking exterior: "The greater part of the palace visible from the ground...consists of a cream-colored oolitic freestone, which, especially on the N. front, has turned to a golden yellow on the surface. This stone is peculiar because it is full of fragments and whole specimens of large fossil sea-urchins or sand-dollars...The steps of the porticoes on both N. and S. fronts are of a dark gray Paleozoic sandstone..."

In this next passage, Every Castle described the symbolism of the palace's themes succinctly: "Blenheim Palace represents the culmination of the English Baroque...It remains the finest expression of Vanbrugh's theatrical style, combining dramatic quality, and a sense of mass and volume with the more intricate details and complex skyline that heralded a more picturesque and Romantic approach. Among the many influences that inspired him were English medieval fortifications (he originally wished the building to be called 'Blenheim Castle'), the classical rhythms of Wren, and the exuberance of the great Italian and French Baroque palaces."

Visitors will also find a rusting cistern above the palace gates. Water for the palace was once stored in this reserve. Servants were made to pump water into the reserve regularly, which traveled to the cistern via a network of oak pipes.

The design of the 1,000 or so windows around the manor is anything but random. Rather, the size of the window dictated one's place in the hierarchy. Floor-length windows were fitted into the walls of master bedrooms. In contrast, the lowliest of servants, such as maids and gardeners, were only permitted small square windows. Higher-ranking servants, such as the Resident Steward, Main Housekeeper, and Butler, were allowed slightly larger round windows.

Between the years of 1696 and 1851, all British households were subjected to so-called "window taxes." These duties were dictated by not only the number of windows, but the size and the amount of sunlight that streamed into one's windows, a bizarre policy that supposedly resulted in the expression "daylight robbery." The following is a general list of the window taxes: "6 windows or fewer – 0; 7-9 windows – 2 shillings (1o pence); 10-19 windows – 4 shillings (20 pence); 20 or more windows – 6 shillings (30 pence)." As a result, the duke and duchess had to shell out 8 shillings (£48.43 today) for Blenheim Palace alone. To dodge the contentious banded tax, citizens cleverly bricked or glazed up all but 6-9 of their windows. Whether or not the Marlborough descendants were concerned about such a tax is uncertain, but it can probably be safely presumed that the thrifty duchess took full advantage of this loophole.

The Resident Steward presided over the 70 servants that dwelled and worked in Blenheim Palace. Their collective salaries alone cost the couple close to £3,000 each year. By the 19th century, the number of servants in Blenheim had trickled up to 80. Though the servants' wages, averaging about £43 (£5,888 today) per annum each, would be considered borderline slavery in this day and age, they were a vast improvement from the compensation Sarah's servants received. The following is a list of the duchess' payroll: "May King (Laundry Maid) £6 (£821) per annum; Anne Middleton (Laundry Maid) £6; Walter Jones (Porter) £8 (£1,095); Necessary Woman (kitchen cleaner, 8 days) 29 pence (£16.57); Washerwoman (2 days) 12.5 pence (£7.12)."

Not only were the servants made to exert themselves around the clock for seven days a week with little rest, all to complete an endless queue of chores in exchange for low pay, working conditions were often problematic. For over a century, servants had to clamber up a narrow and wobbly spiral staircase to reach the top of the clock tower, where they were made to set and adjust the time. Today, this task is performed mechanically. Similarly, since the duke's flag was flown only when he was physically in the palace, servants also had to lower and fetch the flag during his absence.

The chaste elegance the duchess so craved was present throughout the palace's interior, but as the years progressed, it was enlivened by her more stylish descendants. Plush velvet carpets in bright, royal hues and fancy patterned rugs were draped over the oak floors. Ornate chandeliers and baroque furniture clothed in elaborate patterns and finished off with gilded trimmings were introduced to the salon, dining hall, bedchambers, and drawing rooms. The bare walls were adorned with colorful tapestries, such as those depicting the duke's victories, framed lifelike portraits of key Marlborough family members, and a curated gallery of artwork by Titian, Raphael, and Rubens.

William Ranken's portrait of the salon

The famous Long Library of Blenheim Palace, which began as a picture gallery in Hawksmoor's time, was remodeled by Charles Spencer, the 3rd Duke of Marlborough and former Earl of Sunderland, to make room for what he dubbed the "Sunderland Library." The Sunderland Library was a precious collection of manuscripts and texts that Charles had inherited from his father, also Charles, the 3rd Earl of Sunderland, transferred to Blenheim from the Sunderland House in Piccadilly in 1749. Much to his disappointment, the new shelves he installed posed numerous problems. The shelves located on the north and south ends, which obstructed old windows, were slowly rotting away from damp, whereas the books on the east wall, directly exposed to sunlight, were at risk of damage and deterioration.

Renovations and additions aside, the majority of the Long Library's design can still be attributed to Hawksmoor. The Sunderland Library was pawned off between the years of 1881 and 1883, and the library briefly reverted to a picture gallery, but the bookshelves on the east wall remained until the early 20th century. In 1912, it was once again reconverted to a library by Charles Spencer-Churchill, the 9th Duke of Marlborough. Apart from the 10,000 books that line the slim space's bookshelves, visitors will also find Rysbrack's busts of the 1st Duke of Marlborough and 3rd Duke of Marlborough.

A picture of the library

The 3rd Duke of Marlborough

The Marlborough successors, particularly the 9th Duke of Marlborough, were also responsible for the glamorous makeovers of a variety of halls and state rooms. The Green Drawing Room, named as such for the lime-green furniture and matching panels on its walls, is embellished with marvelous tapestries and a portrait of George Spencer, 4th Duke of Marlborough. The most breathtaking parts of this room are the sculptural ornaments of eagles and the dainty accents on the edges of the ceiling, made of pure gold.

The 9th Duke of Marlborough

Likewise, the Red Drawing Room is covered in rich, red wallpaper, and displays a number of Marlborough family portraits. The complementary stools, chaise longues, and century appropriate furniture in "mid-Georgian, English Rocco, and Neoclassical styles," were curated by the reputable London-based cabinet maker Thomas Chippendale.

The overall landscaping of Blenheim Palace was the work of Lancelot "Capability" Brown at the behest of George, the 4th Duke of Marlborough, in 1763. It seems he had the scenic gardens of the Versailles in mind, and as instructed by George in a letter written on June 29 that year, Brown was to prioritize his work at the Blenheim Palace above all his other ongoing projects.

Brown would not disappoint. He added to the blank canvas of space a sparkling 40 acre lake fringed by dense trees, a pair of dams, and winding drives. For his work at Blenheim Palace, Brown was awarded £24 per annum, or £41,720 today.

The 9th Duke of Marlborough would later shower Brown with overdue praises: "The Lake was made by a consummate artist. The contours are good, the ground has been made to undulate; a convex band on one side finds its vis-a-vis with a concave bank on the other side. All this done with the skill of the Romantic period, and on a scale bigger than the Basin des Suisses..."

The detail Brown injected into his work was what gave him not only his green thumb, but a golden touch. The breeds of the trees, as well as their harmonious placements, were some of his primary concerns. The balance of the mixed fragrances produced by the trees and the positioning of the trees around pedestrian paths, he believed, could either repel or entice one to further stroll through the pleasure gardens and appreciate them to their fullest extent. The palace's assemblage of trees – acacia, oak, cedar, chestnut, poplar, and beech, amongst others – were prettiest in autumn.

Brown's official website describes the vibrant biodiversity within the palace: "At Blenheim, the parkland supports a variety of habitats including ancient woodland, replanted ancient woodland, lowland calcareous grassland, coastal floodplain grazing march, deciduous woodland, mixed coniferous woodland, traditional orchards, and reedbeds around the lakes which provide habitats for a variety of insects, butterflies, and moths, as well as otter and water vole."

The Orangery, which housed the first Clock Tower, was introduced as a greenhouse for orange trees during its debut. Towards the latter half of the 18th century, however, the 4th Duke of Marlborough transformed the Orangery into an opulent auditorium filled with 200 seats, all to indulge his young children, who enjoyed writing, directing, and performing their own plays.

It was the 9th Duke of Marlborough who commissioned the French landscape architect, Achille Duchene, to design the Water Terrace. This plot of land was initially flat, so dozens of workers had to be brought in to burrow through the ground and extract over 675,000 cubic feet of earth. Only then could the varying levels visible today be set in place.

In essence, the terrace was a box-shaped piece bordered by manicured hedges. In the center of the box was a perfectly round fountain-pool, surrounded by a quartet of smaller fountain-pools in free-form shapes, and four semi-trefoil pools. The spaces between these pools were filled with mesmerizing labyrinthine hedges. The water in the pools came from Rosamund's Well.

A Legacy Like No Other

"The problems of victory are more agreeable than those of defeat, but they are no less difficult." – attributed to Prime Minister Winston Churchill

In the centuries that followed, royals and dignitaries from near and far traveled to Oxfordshire to visit the legendary Blenheim Palace. "We have nothing equal to this," King George III mused to Queen Charlotte upon his first visit in 1786. Other royals who took the time to tour the grand estate included the King of Denmark in 1768, the Emperor of Russia in 1814, Queen Adelaide of Saxe-Meiningen in 1835, and Prince Albert in 1841. Edward VII, the Prince of Wales, journeyed to the palace in 1859, and he revisited the palace on three separate occasions between 1870 and 1896.

Be that as it may, it did not take long for the Marlborough descendants to realize that their ancestors had possibly bitten off more than they could chew. The 1st Duke of Marlborough was part of the nouveau riche, and as such, he had trouble curbing his decadent spending. Much of the £50,000 fortune he had left behind was poured into the construction of the palace, leaving just a few thousands for his heir. Nonetheless, his descendants continued to live rather cozily, teetering between the upper-middle class and the lower upper-class for years.

This changed in the early 19th century when the palace was inherited by George Spencer-Churchill, the 5th Duke of Marlborough. To put it lightly, he had expensive tastes and virtually no understanding of budget control. The younger George was positively smitten with the gardens installed by the previous duke, and he dedicated a lot of his time to enhancing the landscape even further. He squandered immense sums on dozens of "specialist" pleasure gardens, the bulk of which have since vanished (except for the Rose Garden), and he also splurged on rare, costly flowers, bushes, and plants, his favorite being orchids. When the family finances eventually ran dry, he had no option but to sell off the dynasty's other properties, as well as his personal library. The prices he accepted reflected the duke's desperation. The Boccaccio Manor, for example, was sold for a measly £875 (£67,150 today).

The 5th Duke of Marlborough

The financial woes inherited by the 6th Duke of Marlborough in the mid-19th century pushed the family towards the edge of bankruptcy. There were barely any funds to cover even the most basic of expenses, let alone the exorbitant maintenance costs. As a result, the building fell into severe neglect. The 6th Duke of Marlborough attempted some damage control by applying for and acquiring a special act granted to him by Parliament that allowed him to rely on timber and mortgage sales to finance repairs for the palace. He would spend a staggering total of £80,000 on rehabilitation alone, a project directed by the architect Thomas Allason.

Repairs commenced in 1841, but progress was further stalled by miscommunication, delays, and other quandaries. When the King of Saxony visited the palace in 1844, he was displeased to find "almost every part [of Blenheim] in disorder." The monarch's accompanying party also took note of the "extravagantly opulent" lifestyle incongruously led by the financially ailing

Marlborough family. Among the peculiarities that stood out to them the most was the fountain unnecessarily installed next to the dairy farm; whereas most others would use the space as an "entrance avenue," the Marlborough family used it as a decorative space first, and a place to cool freshly-churned butter and milk second.

The Marlborough successors struggled to keep their finances afloat throughout the 1870s. In 1875, the 7th Duke of Marlborough, who failed to reverse the family's fast depleting fortunes, gathered a number of family treasures, including a 16th century painting entitled "Marriage of Cupid and Psyche" and a chest of the invaluable Marlborough gems, and parted with them at an auction for £10,000.

Those funds were ultimately insufficient to support the family for long. Five years later, the 7th Duke of Marlborough acquired another decree from Parliament – the Blenheim Settled Estates Act of 1880 – which effectively canceled the government's ownership over certain items inside the estate. Another wholesale auction was organized, and this one saw the aforementioned sale of the Sunderland Library for £60,000. In that auction, a 15th century edition of *The Epistles of Horace* and a collection of works by Josephus were among the 18,000 books sold. The Raphael original, *Ansidei Madonna*, soon followed suit, auctioned off at a price of £70,000, followed by Anthony van Dyck's *Equestrian Portrait of Charles I* for £17,500. The family also had to sell off one of Rubens' paintings, which had been gifted to the 1st Duke of Marlborough by the city of Brussels.

When the 9th Duke of Marlborough took custody of Blenheim Palace in 1892, he inherited the family's deflated finances. Fearing the loss of the family legacy, as well as one of the inimitable jewels of British history, Charles vowed to turn things around. For help, he would find Consuelo Vanderbilt, a member of "Commodore" Cornelius Vanderbilt's family and one of the most eligible American women of her era. It was not a fate chosen by Consuelo, but her status-yearning mother, Alva, who urged her to take a European member of the aristocracy as her husband. Charles was in a similar position; he came from one of the most revered lineages in all of Britain, but was seriously strapped for cash. To Alva, they were a match made in heaven.

Consuelo Vanderbilt

In November 1895 (according to some sources, 1896), Charles and Consuelo exchanged their vows at Manhattan's St. Thomas' Episcopal Church, and upon their return, the duke wasted no time in initiating a succession of repairs, renovations, and redecorations on the palace. Charles retrieved numerous family treasures, reacquired a few of the paintings, purchased several new pieces, and refilled the desolate halls and state rooms with a medley of new furniture. In time, he would help restore the palace to at least a modicum of its past glory.

The entrepreneurial marriage of the incompatible Charles and Consuelo was critical to the Marlborough family history in more ways than one. Future Prime Minister Winston Churchill was originally next to inherit the title of Duke of Marlborough, but in 1897, the birth of the couple's eldest son, John Albert William Spencer-Churchill, knocked Winston out of the running. This helped motivate him to seek his fortunes elsewhere, including in politics.

Consuelo and Winston Churchill in 1902

The Vanderbilt dowry, which amounted to $2.5 million USD (£52 million today), coupled with the additional annual allowance of $100,000 granted to the couple by William Vanderbilt, ensured the 9th Duke of Marlborough and his wife were set for life. That being said, they pined for the companionship of others from the very beginning and were deeply unhappy with each other. This was clear even on the day of their wedding, as a passage from Consuelo's diary indicates:"I spent the morning of my wedding day in tears and alone; no one came near me. A footman had been posted at the door of my apartment and not even my governess was admitted. Like an automaton, I donned the lovely lingerie with its real lace and the white silk stockings and shoes...[but] I felt cold and numb as I went down to meet my father and the bridesmaids who were waiting for me..."

Consuelo despised the fact that her husband cared more about his beloved manor than he did about her. Apart from their lack of common interests, Charles was to Consuelo cold, ill-tempered, and unduly obsessed with the Marlborough reputation. Consuelo was apparently so nauseated with her husband that she insisted upon using a large, silver vessel – an heirloom carved with an illustration of the 1st Duke at the Battle of Blenheim – as the centerpiece for their dining table. She nicknamed the heirloom her "cache-man," meaning "hide the husband," as it acted as a wall between her and Charles, who was seated at the opposite end of the table.

On top of all her other grievances, Consuelo loathed the palace with a passion. She groused about her husband's choice in furniture, found fault in his eye for art, and lamented over the absence of hot water and central heating. The brooding duchess spent most of her days cooped up in the only tolerable parts of the palace, and her private journals and memoirs hinted at her depression. One such excerpt reads, "From my window, I overlooked a pond in which a former butler had drowned himself. As one gloomy day succeeded another, I began to feel a deep sympathy for him."

After 26 miserable years, the disconsolate couple finally parted ways, with their divorce finalized in 1921. Charles subsequently married Gladys Deacon, once a friend of Consuelo's, and she was to Charles everything that Consuelo wasn't. While both women were graced with similarly soft and delicate good looks, Gladys, a tortured, but beautiful soul with a tragic past and a lust for art, was ambitious, conversational, and infinitely intriguing. Gladys also took the initiative to leave her own unique imprint on the palace. In 1928, she commissioned the mural specialist Colin Gill to paint three surreal, "masonic" sets of eyes unto the ceiling of the Great North Portico. All six mimicked the shape of Gladys' eyes and were set against bursts of light, but half of the pupils were hazel in color and the other three were in blue.

A portrait of Gladys

World War I and World War II played important roles in the history of the palace. Not only did John Albert, then the Marquess of Blanford, enlist in the British Army during the First World War, the officials and servants of Blenheim Palace went above and beyond to fulfill their patriotic duties. In the summer of 1914, the 9th Duke of Marlborough established the Women's Land Corps, which eventually evolved into the Women's Land Army. At the same time, he locked the open doors of the palace's main entrance with door stops and converted the Long Library to a convalescent ward, which could house at least 50 soldiers at a time.

The palace's makeshift hospital, which came equipped with a surgical ward, a reading room, and even a smoking area, began its service in September of that year. It was staffed with at least two local doctors and a small band of nurses who diligently catered to their patients, day in and day out. Neighboring chemists and shop owners also dropped in about once a week to restock the supplies. Additionally, the 9th Duke of Marlborough's sister and fellow resident of the Blenheim Palace joined in on the war effort by journeying to France and erecting a hospital there.

The sense of community within the palace during its direst times was at its pinnacle. Maids, cooks, and other servants bustled back and forth without stop, cooking and cleaning for, and washing the bloodied clothes of wounded soldiers. Other neighbors sent in gift baskets brimming with fruits, vegetables, meat, and edible packaged goods, as well as bundles of clothes and bed jackets.

Arthur Hine was another courageous member of the palace's extended family. Arthur was an intelligent young estate clerk who was supposedly appointed the "eyes and ears" (in other words, a spy) for Winston Churchill, then a general. As Winston's inside man, Arthur reportedly zipped through the Belgian city of Antwerp on his motorcycle during the days of its bombardment, collecting intelligence that was as consequential as it was confidential. There, he rescued a young child from a blazing cellar and brought her back home to England, where his parents raised her as their own daughter. Arthur ultimately survived the war, but he would suffer from severe PTSD and could never bring himself to set foot in the palace again.

The convalescent ward in Blenheim Palace remained in service until the end of May 1915. Interestingly, although the war had brought everyone together, it was this same war that ripped apart innumerable families. The casualties of the war led the nation to sink into a deep depression, both in terms of morale and economy, and like Arthur, many of the palace's staff members refused to return to the estate. The dismal duke watched as financially ruined neighbors sold off mansions and tracts of land that had belonged to their families for centuries. Rather than slow down on his spending, however, this compelled the duke to embellish and preserve the Marlborough estate with a revitalized zest, so as to strengthen the family legacy even further.

In September 1940, the palace opened its doors once again when the family permitted authorities to transform a section of the estate into a MI5 base, though not without some friction. Helen Oin, who was stationed at Blenheim Palace during this time, detailed her experience there: "Our stay at Wormwood Scrubs despite intricate air raid shelters was abruptly ended when the building was bombed...so Churchill in his wisdom decided that our next residence should be Blenheim Palace...We had three huts and were beside the courtyard which contained four squares of sacred soil brought back from the site of the Battle of Blenheim. The [10th] Duke of Marlborough was insistent that nobody should walk on the soil, but he was not a match for the removal men who when they found that they were carrying cupboards full of ashes, walked straight across the sacred soil."

Moreover, the Long Library was transformed into a shelter for 400 displaced schoolboys from Malvern College. The estate, at this point, could only be described as organized mayhem. Servants harvested fruit and vegetables from the Formal Gardens and delivered them to the cooks in the sweltering kitchen as others scrubbed plates and beddings. Some were busy transporting weapons, equipment, and supplies across the estate, while others boarded up the windows and entrances of the palace. Meanwhile, soldiers completed obstacle courses and carried out drills over the lake.

Blenheim Palace was reopened to the public in 1950, about five years after World War II, and it became an immediate hotspot for crowds, a trend that continues today. In 1957, the estate was classed as a "Grade-I listed building," and the manor was formally recognized as a UNESCO World Heritage Site in 1987. By then, it was receiving an average of 350,000 unique visitors each year. The palace remains in the custody of the Duke of Marlborough to this day.

In October, 2014, the estate was passed down to the 58-year-old Charles James Blanford Spencer-Churchill, the 12th Duke of Marlborough. National papers mentioned the transition in its headlines for days, sensationalizing not only the peeling back of a new chapter, but the troubled past of the new duke, one marred by violence and crime. Jamie was the stark opposite of his seemingly saintly father, the 11th Duke of Marlborough, whom many have lauded as the second savior of Blenheim Palace. Conversely, Jamie was a convicted serial criminal with a past addiction to heroin and cocaine. His narcotic binges and debauched escapades, amongst other flaws, became so unmanageable that at one point, his father took him to court in 1994 in an attempt to permanently disown him. After all, the £100 million estate and the very future of the dukedom were at stake.

Only after Jamie entered himself into rehab did the pair finally mend their issues. The elderly 11th Duke of Marlborough, following a change of heart, agreed to leave the estate in Jamie's custody, but the 12th Duke of Marlborough was to govern the palace alongside a board of trustees, all of whom were vested with the power of a veto. John Spencer-Churchill, the 11th Duke of Marlborough, explained, "I am fully confident that James will be able to keep this place going. But over the top of him – and over the top of me – are trustees. You can't predict the future." Today, the trustees consist of two separate entities: Blenheim Trustee Company Limited 1 and Blenheim Trustee Company Limited 2.

As all of this suggests, conserving and protecting the family's greatest legacy continues to be critically important to those at the head of the family. As the 11th Duke of Marlborough put it so well, "Trying to keep Blenheim going is a very important part of the family's history and life at the present time, and so what we're trying to do is ensure that Blenheim is kept for future generations...Although the Battle of Blenheim was won in 1704, the Battle for Blenheim continues in the unceasing struggle to maintain the structure of the building, and to obtain the finance for the future..."

Online Resources

Other books about British history by Charles River Editors

Other books about the Blenheim Palace on Amazon

Further Reading

Editors, R. *Blenheim Palace*. 4 Sept. 2018, www.revolvy.com/page/Blenheim-Palace. Accessed 13 Sept. 2018.

Editors, A I. *Blenheim Palace: 300 Years of Captivating Tales*. 17 Apr. 2018, antennainternational.com/blenheim-palace-300-years-of-captivating-tales/. Accessed 13 Sept. 2018.

Baggs, A P, et al. *Blenheim: Blenheim Palace*. 1990, www.british-history.ac.uk/vch/oxon/vol12/pp448-460. Accessed 13 Sept. 2018.

Editors, H R. *Blenheim Palace, Oxfordshire*. 2017, www.hauntedrooms.co.uk/blenheim-palace. Accessed 13 Sept. 2018.

Editors, B B. *Blenheim Palace: 'Mysterious Vaults' Found by Stonemasons*. 13 June 2017, www.bbc.com/news/uk-england-oxfordshire-40264213. Accessed 13 Sept. 2018.

Editors, B B. *Blenheim Palace Flowerpot Turns out to Be Roman Coffin*. 9 Mar. 2017, www.bbc.com/news/uk-england-oxfordshire-39216040. Accessed 13 Sept. 2018.

Editors, B E. *Blenheim Palace*. 2017, www.britainexpress.com/counties/oxfordshire/houses/Blenheim.htm. Accessed 13 Sept. 2018.

Pipe, S. *General Features - Blenheim Palace*. 23 Oct. 2007, www.bbc.co.uk/oxford/content/articles/2007/10/17/glyme_feature.shtml. Accessed 13 Sept. 2018.

Wayland, M J. *Royalist Devil of Woodstock*. 18 Dec. 2012, mjwayland.com/royalist-devil-of-woodstock/. Accessed 13 Sept. 2018.

Editors, J F. *Interesting Facts about Blenheim Palace*. 2017, justfunfacts.com/interesting-facts-about-blenheim-palace/. Accessed 13 Sept. 2018.

Editors, G O. *INTERESTING FACTS ABOUT BLENHEIM PALACE*. 2017, getoutside.ordnancesurvey.co.uk/guides/facts-about-blenheim-palace/. Accessed 13 Sept. 2018.

Editors, H E. *10 Things You Might Not Know about Blenheim Palace – the 'Real Downton Abbey.'* Oct. 2014, www.historyextra.com/period/stuart/blenheim-palace-real-downton-abbey-donald-trump-facts-uk-visit/. Accessed 13 Sept. 2018.

Rabon, J. *Great Houses: 10 Interesting Facts and Figures about Blenheim Palace – The Birthplace of Winston Churchill*. 26 Jan. 2015, www.anglotopia.net/british-history/great-houses-10-interesting-facts-figures-blenheim-palace-birthplace-winston-churchill/. Accessed 13 Sept. 2018.

Editors, I T. *Blenheim Palace: Some Intriguing Facts*. 17 Feb. 2014, theitchtotravel.wordpress.com/2014/02/17/blenheim-palace-some-intriguing-facts/. Accessed 13 Sept. 2018.

Reginato, J. *Magnificent Obsession*. June 2011, www.vanityfair.com/news/2011/06/blenheim-palace-201106. Accessed 13 Sept. 2018.

Dawson, S. *A Brief History of Blenheim Palace*. 23 Aug. 2017, theculturetrip.com/europe/united-kingdom/england/articles/a-brief-history-of-blenheim-palace/. Accessed 13 Sept. 2018.

Editors, B P. *History of Blenheim Palace*. 2018, www.blenheimpalace.com/visit-us/the-palace/history/. Accessed 13 Sept. 2018.

David, S. *Marlborough, Britain's Greatest General*. 18 July 2008, www.telegraph.co.uk/culture/books/non_fictionreviews/3553912/Marlborough-Britains-greatest-general.html. Accessed 13 Sept. 2018.

Editors, E C. *Marlborough, John Churchill, 1st Duke Of*. 2011, www.encyclopedia.com/people/history/british-and-irish-history-biographies/john-churchill-1st-duke-marlborough. Accessed 13 Sept. 2018.

Editors, E C. *Spanish Succession, War Of The*. 2015, www.encyclopedia.com/history/modern-europe/wars-and-battles/war-spanish-succession#1E1SpanSuc. Accessed 14 Sept. 2018.

Editors, N W. *John Churchill*. 15 May 2014, www.newworldencyclopedia.org/entry/John_Churchill. Accessed 14 Sept. 2018.

Editors, Y D. *1st Duke of Marlborough Facts*. 2010, biography.yourdictionary.com/1st-duke-of-marlborough. Accessed 14 Sept. 2018.

Editors, U N. *John Churchill, 1st Duke of Marlborough (1650-1722; Army Officer and Politician)*. 2017, www.nottingham.ac.uk/manuscriptsandspecialcollections/learning/biographies/johnchurchill,1st dukeofmarlborough(1650-1722).aspx. Accessed 14 Sept. 2018.

Trueman, C N. *John Churchill, Duke of Marlborough*. 17 Mar. 2015, www.historylearningsite.co.uk/stuart-england/john-churchill-duke-of-marlborough/. Accessed 14 Sept. 2018.

Editors, A T. *Great Britons: John Churchill 1st Duke of Marlborough – The Man Who Redrew the Map of Europe and Inspired Winston Churchill*. 1 Apr. 2015, www.anglotopia.net/british-history/great-britons-john-churchill-1st-duke-of-marlborough-the-man-who-redrew-the-map-of-europe-and-inspired-winston-churchill/. Accessed 14 Sept. 2018.

Twinney, D. *Notable Names: John Churchill, Duke of Marlborough*. 26 Jan. 2015, royalcentral.co.uk/blogs/history/notable-names-john-churchill-duke-of-marlborough-43619. Accessed 14 Sept. 2018.

Millikan, R. *BLENHEIM PALACE: Woodstock, UK* . 2017, www.travelwriterstales.com/16-blenheim.htm. Accessed 14 Sept. 2018.

Southey, R. *THE BATTLE OF BLENHEIM*. 2004, www.poetry-archive.com/s/the_battle_of_blenheim.html. Accessed 14 Sept. 2018.

Editors, L M. *Sarah Churchill, Duchess of Marlborough*. 2017, www.liverpoolmuseums.org.uk/collections/lgbt/love-and-relationships/queer-relationships/queen-anne-and-sarah-churchill/item-227538.aspx. Accessed 14 Sept. 2018.

Dowd, V. *The Woman behind Queen Anne's Reign*. 29 Nov. 2015, www.bbc.com/news/entertainment-arts-34957424. Accessed 14 Sept. 2018.

Domin, H. *Great Loves in History: 'An Immoderate Passion': Queen Anne of Great Britain and Sarah Churchill, Duchess of Marlborough*. 14 Feb. 2012, unusualhistoricals.blogspot.com/2012/02/great-loves-in-history-immoderate.html. Accessed 14 Sept. 2018.

Zuvich, A. *'Pray Stay Till Sunday' – Queen Anne's Letters to Sarah Churchill, Guest Post by Joanne Limburg*. 17 May 2015, www.andreazuvich.com/history/pray-stay-till-sunday-queen-annes-letters-to-sarah-churchill-guest-post-by-joanne-limburg/. Accessed 14 Sept. 2018.

Morpeth, C. *The Great Lesbian Queen Anne?* 13 Dec. 2013, fourtwonine.com/2013/12/13/3661-the-great-lesbian-queen-anne/. Accessed 14 Sept. 2018.

Editors, H M. *The Power Behind Two Thrones: Sarah Churchill, Duchess of Marlborough (1660-1744)*. 21 Sept. 2012, historicmusings.blogspot.com/2012/09/the-power-behind-two-thrones-sarah.html. Accessed 14 Sept. 2018.

Turchyn, K. *Blenheim Palace: A Gift from a Queen*. 24 Sept. 2015, royalcentral.co.uk/residences/blenheim-palace-a-gift-from-a-queen-53866. Accessed 14 Sept. 2018.

Edge, S. *Winston Churchill's Racy Relatives*. 23 Apr. 2011, www.express.co.uk/expressyourself/242377/Winston-Churchill-s-racy-relatives. Accessed 14 Sept. 2018.

Pointon, M. *MATERIAL MANOEUVRES: SARAH CHURCHILL, DUCHESS OF MARLBOROUGH AND THE POWER OF ARTEFACTS*. June 2009, library.pcw.gov.ph/sites/default/files/material manoeuvres, sarah churchill.pdf. Accessed 17 Sept. 2018.

Harris, F. *ACCOUNTS OF THE CONDUCT OF SARAH, DUCHESS OF MARLBOROUGH, 1704-1742*. 2017, www.bl.uk/eblj/1982articles/pdf/article2.pdf. Accessed 17 Sept. 2018.

Johnson, B. *Blenheim Palace*. 2017, www.historic-uk.com/HistoryMagazine/DestinationsUK/Blenheim-Palace/. Accessed 17 Sept. 2018.

Editors, C. *The History of the Royal Manor of Woodstock and Blenheim Palace* . 10 Aug. 2018, www.cotswolds.info/places/woodstock/history.shtml. Accessed 17 Sept. 2018.

Editors, U E. *Architectural History of Blenheim Palace*. 1 May 2018, www.ukessays.com/essays/architecture/architectural-history-of-blenheim-palace.php. Accessed 17 Sept. 2018.

Herman, R. *SARAH AND HER ARCHITECTS*. 6 Mar. 2016, www.hertsmemories.org.uk/content/herts-history/people/hertfordshire-centenarians/sarah-and-her-architects. Accessed 17 Sept. 2018.

Field, O. *The Favourite: Sarah, Duchess of Marlborough*. 21 Sept. 2002, www.smh.com.au/entertainment/books/the-favourite-sarah-duchess-of-marlborough-20020921-gdfnh7.html. Accessed 17 Sept. 2018.

Editors, W. *Blenheim Palace, Oxfordshire - Part 1*. 2017, wasleys.org.uk/eleanor/stately_homes_castles/england/westmidlands/blenheim/blenheim_one/index.html. Accessed 17 Sept. 2018.

Smith, E. *BLENHEIM PALACE: THE GRANDEST PRIVATE RESIDENCE THAT OUTSHINES THE BRITISH MONARCHY'S HOMES*. 21 Aug. 2016, elnasmith.wordpress.com/2016/08/21/blenheim-palace-the-grandest-private-residence-that-outshines-the-british-monarchys-homes/. Accessed 17 Sept. 2018.

Editors, A A. *The Decorated Duchess*. 5 June 2013, www.armchairanglophile.com/the-decorated-duchess/. Accessed 17 Sept. 2018.

Venning, A. *Britain's Bisexual Queen: New Film Explores the Secret Passion between Queen Anne and Her Right-Hand Woman before Their Affair Descended into Fury and Blackmail*. 25 June 2017, www.dailymail.co.uk/news/article-4636386/The-secret-passion-Queen-Anne-Sarah-Churchill.html. Accessed 17 Sept. 2018.

Editors, B P. *BLENHEIM PALACE HOME OF THE 11TH DUKE OF MARLBOROUGH*. 2017, www.blenheimpalace.com/assets/files/images/education/downloads/Courtyard Capers.pdf. Accessed 17 Sept. 2018.

Moore, H. *Edward I Strong*. 2008, liberty.henry-moore.org/henrymoore/sculptor/browserecord.php?-action=browse&-recid=2609. Accessed 17 Sept. 2018.

Editors, R. *John Vanbrugh*. 20 Aug. 2018, www.revolvy.com/page/John-Vanbrugh. Accessed 17 Sept. 2018.

Ross, D. *John Vanbrugh Biography*. 2017, www.britainexpress.com/History/bio/vanbrugh.htm. Accessed 17 Sept. 2018.

Editors, C W. *Blenheim Palace: The Untold Story*. 2018, www.cotswoldswebsite.com/blenheimpalace/. Accessed 17 Sept. 2018.

Cartwright, M. *The Arch of Titus, Rome*. 16 June 2013, www.ancient.eu/article/499/the-arch-of-titus-rome/. Accessed 17 Sept. 2018.

Editors, W S. *Text on the Column of Victory in the Grounds of Blenheim Palace*. 12 Mar. 2018, en.wikisource.org/wiki/Text_on_the_Column_of_Victory_in_the_grounds_of_Blenheim_Palace. Accessed 18 Sept. 2018.

Editors, H E. *COLUMN OF VICTORY*. 2016, historicengland.org.uk/listing/the-list/list-entry/1368002. Accessed 18 Sept. 2018.

Editors, C P. *Blenheim Palace - The Victory Column*. 13 June 2015, www.cheriesplace.me.uk/blog/index.php/2015/06/13/blenheim-palace-the-victory-column/. Accessed 18 Sept. 2018.

Editors, B H. *Blenheim: Woodstock Manor*. 2018, www.british-history.ac.uk/vch/oxon/vol12/pp431-435. Accessed 18 Sept. 2018.

Editors, E C. *Blenheim Palace*. 2016, www.everycastle.com/Blenheim-Palace.html. Accessed 18 Sept. 2018.

Wiseman, K. *BLENHEIM PALACE*. 2017, www.capabilitybrown.org/garden/blenheim-palace. Accessed 18 Sept. 2018.

Arkell, W J. *The Building-Stones of Blenheim Palace, Cornbury Park, Glympton Park and Heythrop House, Oxfordshire*. 2017, oxoniensia.org/volumes/1948/arkell.pdf. Accessed 18 Sept. 2018.

Editors, B P. *Architecture*. 2018, www.blenheimpalace.com/visit-us/education-team/resources/architecture.html. Accessed 18 Sept. 2018.

Editors, G V. *Blenheim Palace Garden*. 2011, www.gardenvisit.com/gardens/blenheim_palace_garden. Accessed 18 Sept. 2018.

Armstrong, K W. *Blenheim Palace's Stunning Parkland and Pleasure Gardens*. 27 Nov. 2012, kathrynwarmstrong.wordpress.com/tag/blenheim-palace-most-famous-winston-churchill-quotes-ephesians-613-river-glyme-english-baroque-unesco-world-heritage-sites/. Accessed 18 Sept. 2018.

Editors, B P. *5th Duke of Marlborough*. 2018, www.blenheimpalace.com/visit-us/education-team/resources/dukes/5th.html. Accessed 18 Sept. 2018.

Vickers, H. *Gladys, Duchess of Marlborough: the Aristocrat with Attitude*. 7 Feb. 2011, www.telegraph.co.uk/culture/art/art-features/8303256/Gladys-Duchess-of-Marlborough-the-aristocrat-with-attitude.html. Accessed 18 Sept. 2018.

Editors, C. *The 'Dollar Princess' and the Duke.* 22 Oct. 2016, www.christies.com/features/The-story-of-Consuelo-Vanderbilts-marriage-to-the-Duke-of-Marlborough-7745-1.aspx. Accessed 18 Sept. 2018.

Editors, V M. *Fortunate Son: Lord Charles Spencer-Churchill Was the Life of the Party.* 26 Feb. 2018, news.vanderbilt.edu/vanderbiltmagazine/fortunate-son-lord-charles-spencer-churchill-was-the-life-of-the-party/. Accessed 18 Sept. 2018.

Howard, V. *The American Heiresses Who Saved the British Aristocracy: Consuelo Vanderbilt, Duchess of Marlborough.* 16 Jan. 2017, www.thecrownchronicles.co.uk/history/history-posts/conseulo-vanderbilt-duchess-of-marlborough-dollar-princess-american-heiress/. Accessed 18 Sept. 2018.

Editors, P. *Little Known Blenheim -The 9th Duke of Malborough.* 18 July 2017, www.penhaligons.com/blog/little-known-blenheim-the-9th-duke-of-malborough/. Accessed 18 Sept. 2018.

Editors, I T. *Blenheim Palace: Great War House.* 2 Oct. 2014, www.itv.com/presscentre/ep1week40/blenheim-palace-great-war-house. Accessed 19 Sept. 2018.

Gordon, A. *From Hell... to the Splendour of Blenheim Palace: Photos Reveal How Winston Churchill's Birthplace Was Turned into a Hospital for Injured WWI Troops.* 20 Mar. 2018, www.dailymail.co.uk/news/article-5522373/Photos-reveal-Blenheim-Palace-hospital-WWI-troops.html. Accessed 19 Sept. 2018.

Furness, H. *How a Servant Became Churchill's 'Eyes and Ears' during the First World War.* 7 Oct. 2014, ww1.canada.com/faces-of-war/how-a-servant-became-churchills-eyes-and-ears-during-the-first-world-war. Accessed 19 Sept. 2018.

Editors, B P. *World War II Espionage & Evacuees: Blenheim Palace and WWII.* 2017, www.blenheimpalace.com/visit-us/education-team/tour/ww2.html. Accessed 19 Sept. 2018.

Editors, F C. *From a Prison to a Palace.* 11 July 2005, www.bbc.co.uk/history/ww2peopleswar/stories/84/a4427084.shtml. Accessed 19 Sept. 2018.

Rayner, G. *Former Drug Addict and Ex-Convict Jamie Blandford Becomes 12th Duke of Marlborough after Father Dies.* 16 Oct. 2014, www.telegraph.co.uk/news/11168207/Former-drug-addict-and-ex-convict-Jamie-Blandford-becomes-12th-Duke-of-Marlborough-after-father-dies.html. Accessed 19 Sept. 2018.

French, A. *Son Inherits 12th Duke of Marlborough Title but Blenheim Palace Stays with Trustees.* 17 Oct. 2014, www.oxfordmail.co.uk/news/top_news/11541289.Son_inherits_12th_Duke_of_Marlborough_title_but_Blenheim_Palace_stays_with_trustees/. Accessed 19 Sept. 2018.

Wood, A. C. (2010). *Military Ghosts*. Amberley Publishing Limited.

Andrews, R. (2010). *Paranormal Oxford*. Amberley Publishing Limited.

Free Books by Charles River Editors

We have brand new titles available for free most days of the week. To see which of our titles are currently free, click on this link.

Discounted Books by Charles River Editors

We have titles at a discount price of just 99 cents everyday. To see which of our titles are currently 99 cents, click on this link.

Made in the USA
Las Vegas, NV
25 October 2021